People at Home

What do people do at home? As the pictures in this book illustrate, they are born, they marry, they die; they dress and wash, quarrel and relax, play games, make music, write bad poetry and sew shirts through the night.

For many centuries artists have painted people at home — capturing the dramatic moments, or simply creating magical pictures out of figures and their surroundings. *People at Home* shows some of the ideas, tricks and oddities of these artists, and compares 'old masters' with modern painters who have tackled the same subjects.

At the back of the book are short biographies of the artists whose work is shown, and some suggestions for finding out more about them.

Dr Patrick Conner is the author of several books and articles about art. He is Keeper of Fine Art at the Royal Pavilion, Art Gallery and Museums, Brighton, England.

Ronald Parkinson is Head of Education at the Victoria and Albert Museum, London

LOOKING AT ART

People at Home

Patrick Conner

Consultant Editor: Ronald Parkinson
Head of Education, Victoria and Albert Museum, London

A MARGARET K. McELDERRY BOOK

Atheneum   1982   New York

Jacket A detail from David Des Granges, *The Saltonstall Family*, which is reproduced in full on page 19.

Frontispiece Hendrick Sorgh, *The Lute Player* (detail), full picture on p.36.

LIBRARY OF CONGRESS CATALOGING IN PUBLICATION DATA

Conner, Patrick.
  People at home.

  (Looking at art)
  "A Margaret K. McElderry Book."
  SUMMARY: Examines great paintings from various
periods and countries which depict men and women at home.
    1. Home in art—Juvenile literature.   2. Painting—
Juvenile literature. [1. Home in art.   2. Painting—
History]   I. Parkinson, Ronald.   II. Title.   III. Series.
ND1460.H65C6   758'.93059   82-1832
ISBN 0-689-50252-4   AACR2

Printed in Italy by
G. Canale & C.S. p.A., Turin
First American Edition

Contents

Looking at Art

Art is for everyone. With the help of a selection of outstanding pictures, combined with lively, down-to-earth discussion, this series shows clearly how rewarding it is to understand and enjoy paintings. Each book takes a theme, looks at the way it has been treated by famous artists from many different countries throughout the ages, and compares in simple language their varied styles and ideas.

Faces

People at Home

People at Work

List of Plates

Mysterious mirrors

A wedding picture

This famous painting, by the Flemish artist Jan van Eyck, shows a finely dressed couple in a bedroom. He wears a superb hat like a giant door-knob; she wears a billowing green gown which makes a rich contrast with the scarlet bed. But this is more than a picture of a man and wife at home; it records their marriage.

Hidden witnesses

The young man, Giovanni Arnolfini, is promising to love and honour his bride. But a marriage needs a witness; and two witnesses can just be seen, in the curved mirror on the wall. The mirror reflects the back of the bride and groom, and two more figures at the door — just where van Eyck must have stood to paint the picture. It seems, then, that one of these figures must be the artist himself, especially since the words 'Jan van Eyck was here 1434' are written in Latin above the mirror.

A dog at the ceremony

This painting is one of the earliest to show a room that we can recognize as real (compare the less realistic room on page 18). It is full of domestic objects, such as the brush hanging near the mirror, the apples by the window, and the shoes (his and hers) on the floor. The single candle reminds us of a church altar; the mirror-frame has ten scenes of the life of Christ; and just as dogs are faithul to their owners, so the little dog here may indicate the Arnolfinis' promise to be faithful to each other. Van Eyck may have included some of these details to make it clear that this is a sacred ceremony.

At the centre of the globe

If the mirror in van Eyck's picture were not curved, we should see in it very little of the room; the more curved the glass, the wider the area

Maurits Escher, *Hand with reflecting globe,* 1935.

it reflects. The modern Dutch artist Maurits Escher has taken this idea even further than van Eyck. He has drawn himself gazing into a mirror which is a complete globe, with surprising results.

An all-round view

The artist's face and the lamp at the centre are reflected normally. Nearer the edges, the walls and objects appear more and more distorted — most of all, the artist's fingers, which in the glass seem more like monstrous tentacles. And we can actually see all four walls of the room at the same time; the wall and bed on the left are in fact opposite the window.

Yet there is nothing unusual about the globe in Escher's print. We can see the same kind of effect in a silvered marble or a globe on a Christmas tree.

Jan van Eyck *(left) The Marriage of Giovanni Arnolfini and Giovanna Cenami,* 1434; *(above)* a close-up of the mirror.

The artist in the palace

A royal family

The Ladies-in-Waiting (or *Las Meninas*) was painted by Diego Velasquez, Court Painter to King Philip IV of Spain. This, however, is a royal picture with a difference.

The room is cool and lofty. Like the room in van Eyck's painting (page 8), it has a mirror on the far wall; and Velasquez probably knew that painting, which was then in the Spanish royal collection. But instead of reflecting the artist, this mirror reflects the two people whom the artist is painting – the King and Queen of Spain. As we look at the picture, we have the same view as they must have had while they posed for the artist.

Water for the princess

Velasquez has painted himself on the left, brush in hand, by his huge canvas. The centre of attention (and well aware of it) is the King's daughter, Margarita. On either side are her ladies-in-waiting, who curtsey; one offers perfumed water. Two more attendants stand in the shadows, and the palace marshal looks on from the doorway. On the right are two dwarfs, one of them teasing a dog which is as large as herself.

Taking a back seat

In most paintings of royal groups, the King and Queen are given the chief positions; but here Velasquez has reversed this tradition by banishing them to the background. For once it is their artist, daughter and servants who take pride of place.

A mental leap

Three hundred years later, another Spanish-born artist, Pablo Picasso, created his own version of Velasquez's masterpiece. What was his purpose? To explore the workings of a painting which fascinated him; and, as he once said, 'to draw the mind in a direction it's not used to, and wake it up'.

The artist rules

In Velasquez's painting the figure of the artist is already the tallest in the picture. But Picasso makes him taller still, and lowers the ceiling until the idea which Velasquez hinted at has become obvious: the artist dominates the scene. For the artist's head Picasso uses a favourite trick of his, joining two views of the face (from the left and from the right) to make up one larger face with a squinting, quizzical expression.

Spanish humour

The other figures are drawn more sketchily. The mirror is reduced to the size of a television screen, with a blurred image in which only the King's moustache stands out. The broad face of the larger dwarf is now a blank with a few dots and dashes, like the face of Charlie Brown in the comic strip. And the powerful dog seems to have turned into Picasso's own dachshund, which he called 'Lump'.

Pablo Picasso, *Las Meninas,* 1957.

(Left) Diego Velasquez, *Las Meninas,* 1656.

11

The art of the game

Battle of wits

It was in the Netherlands that artists first began to produce paintings of people at home, working, playing or occupied in familiar actions, without any religious or moral message. Jan van Eyck's picture of the Arnolfinis (page 8) was one of the earliest paintings of this kind; another early example is *The Card Players* by the sixteenth-century Dutch artist Lucas van Leyden.

The game which Lucas has portrayed is clearly more than a light-hearted family amusement. Nine men and women are clustered round the table; their fine clothes and powerful colours add glamour to the occasion. No doubt they are betting for high stakes, and the game has reached a critical point. All the players are in deadly earnest.

Poker faces

The couple beneath the window are studying their cards, but the rest of the people seem to be keeping a watchful eye on one another. We can imagine what might be passing through their minds (Is he bluffing? Whose side is she on? Does he hold the ace?). But although the players are occupied with themselves, the eye of the spectator is drawn inwards by the three long, splendid, tilting hats, which point down to what is surely at the back of all the players' minds — the heaps of golden coins which gleam against the dark green tablecloth.

Lucas van Leyden, *The Card Players*, c.1514.

Time to relax

A joke and a chat

The mood of the second painting of card players is lighter. The contest itself seems less serious, for of the figures at the table, only the woman is intent on the game; the three gentlemen around her are joking, smoking and drinking. Pieces of a broken clay pipe can be seen on the tiled floor, but a maid is bringing fresh pipes and a jug of wine across the courtyard.

Space and light

The artist, Pieter de Hooch, was once again a Dutchman. He was at work a century and a half later than Lucas, and he chose to arrange his picture in a very different way. Instead of crowding his card-players up to the edge of the picture, de Hooch has made them occupy no more than a quarter of his canvas. He has placed them in a clean, spacious room, with a tall window and an open door which allow sunlight to stream through on to most of the right-hand wall and the floor. We feel that this carefully defined room, with its many squares and rectangles, is de Hooch's main concern; the players bring contrasting curves and splashes of colour and add to the pleasantly relaxed atmosphere of the scene.

Pieter de Hooch,
The Card Players,
1658.

Catching the eye

Any artist who wants to paint a number of people in a room is faced with a problem: what is to be the centre of attention? If all the characters are shown occupying themselves in their own ways, there is a danger that our eye may flit from one figure to another, unable to find a resting point.

Family group

One solution to the problem is to include a game in the picture — as the French artist Henri Matisse has done in this painting of his family.

The figures are his wife (on the left), his daughter Marguerite (on the right) and his sons Pierre and Jean (in the centre). The two women are turned inwards, directing our attention to the boys sitting between them; and between the boys is the chequered board, on which they are playing checkers. The game forms a focus of interest for the figures in the picture, and for us.

A strong check

The chequer-board catches our eye for a second reason: it is the strongest, most tightly-knit pattern in a room full of patterns, on walls, fireplace, sofas and carpet. In fact the room is not intended simply as a background, but as a decorative arrangement of shapes and colours, which uses the figures as part of that arrangement. The unreal-looking clothes of Matisse's children are painted in flat, all-over colours to contrast with the jiggling of spots and squares all round them.

Henri Matisse, *The Painter's Family,* 1911.

Black and white

In *The Domino Players*, by the American artist Horace Pippin, the game again plays a major part, linking the figures and making a striking pattern of its own. In this case the white spots on the black dominoes are balanced by the black-on-white dotted blouse of the player on the right, and the black-on-red dotted headscarf of the player opposite.

In the kitchen

Horace Pippin was a black artist, brought up in a family which was much poorer than Matisse's, as we would imagine from the bare floor-boards and peeling plaster in the picture. Matisse depicted a comfortable drawing-room, but Pippin set his game in a kitchen; for when he was young, the kitchen was the only living-room for many poor families.

Fighting back

Pippin taught himself to paint. In the First World War a bullet paralysed his right hand, but this did not stop him: he would paint through the night supporting his right wrist with his left hand. Only in his last years did others begin to appreciate his careful style of painting, which followed no artistic fashion but gave his own sharp view of black American life.

Horace Pippin, *The Domino Players*, 1943.

The Shell Game

In an airy room the Shell Game is being played by a group of women. The inside of each of the shells is decorated with either a poem or a painting, and the players' task is to pick out a pair in which the poem and the painting match each other.

Pictures and poems

This print is the work of the Japanese artist Kitagawa Utamaro, whose drawing of slender and graceful women was admired not only in Japan but in Europe after his death. It comes from a book called *Gifts of the Ebb-tide*, in which poems and pictures are printed together on each double page. The first page in the book shows a number of people collecting shells on a beach while the tide is out; the shells themselves appear on the next pages; and *Women playing the Shell Game* — the last picture in the book — shows how the shells were used when the collectors returned home.

Wheels within wheels

Could there ever have been such a scene? The more we look at the picture, the more unreal and dreamlike it appears. There is no sunlight or shade; at the bottom of the picture, the pine-needles and cherry blossom hardly overlap their main branches, as they would in real trees, because Utamaro has wanted to display the branches' twisting shapes. All the parts of the picture create patterns of various kinds. The shells are arranged in circles, and are themselves surrounded by flowers — on the women's dresses, on the painted screens at the right, and on the trees below. And the squiggling characters of the Japanese poem make their own pattern above.

The year of the dog

There are also interesting little features to be found in the corners of the picture. Out on the verandah, a towel-stand and a jug cast shadows on to the screen-wall beside them. On the left a dog rides on an attendant's shoulders, and cranes its neck in just the same way as the woman in black at the centre of the picture. Utamaro may have included this animal for another

reason: to show that the picture was produced in 1790, which is a 'Year of the Dog' in the Japanese calendar.

Kitagawa Utamaro, *Women playing the Shell Game* (details), c.1790.

Birth and death

A special occasion

The events of birth and death often take place in bedrooms, and in these two pictures stately beds occupy a central position. The first, which was painted for a church in the fifteenth century, shows the birth of the Virgin Mary. The artist's name is not known, but since he was German he naturally pictured the room and its furniture as they might have appeared in a wealthy German household of his own time. The actions of the women are beautifully drawn. One takes the newly-born Mary from her mother; another pours water for her bath; another dips her slender fingers into the bowl, to make sure that the water is not too hot; another passes a towel from the linen-chest.

A golden backdrop

Behind the heads of the standing women, where we should expect to see the upper part of the wall or perhaps a window, there is simply a broad, blank area of gold. This artist, like many other European artists before him, was not trying to make every part of his picture look as real as possible; his main purpose was to give a clear idea of each event, as it was told in the Bible or in Christian tradition, and to add a background of gold leaf, a precious material fit for such miraculous stories.

(Above) Master of the Life of the Virgin, *Birth of the Virgin*, c.1460.

Obvious — but wrong

What is happening in the second picture, *The Saltonstall Family?* When it was bought by the Tate Gallery in 1976, the answer seemed obvious: the father was bringing his two eldest children to the bedside of his wife, who was reaching out to welcome them. She, it was said, lay weak and pale because she had just delivered her third child, seen in the arms of a relation on the right.

Death in the family

But it has now been discovered that this painting is not about birth at all. The father, Sir Richard Saltonstall, is certainly visiting his wife's bedside, but she lies dead; the artist has painted her arm outstretched to show that the children on the left were her own. The woman in the chair is Sir Richard's second wife, whom he married three years after his first wife died, and she is the mother of the baby she holds.

An extra wife

So the artist (named David Des Granges) painted a group of people who were never actually together. He wanted to make a record of the whole family, which had to include both wives — the first dead, the second alive. But it is still a tender scene. Sir Richard has taken off one glove to hold the hand of his eldest child (a boy), while he looks down at the baby, forming a link between his first family and his second.

David Des Granges, *The Saltonstall Family*, c.1637.

Reading for pleasure

A quiet moment

Nothing is unusual in the subject of *A Young Girl Reading*, by the French artist Fragonard. There is no story for us to guess at, and no particular connection between the artist and the model who posed for the picture. It is simply a marvellous piece of painting; and as the subject is familiar and uncomplicated, there is nothing to distract us from the painter's art.

Riot of curves

The picture is made up almost completely of curves. In the girl's hair, face and body, and in the plump, inviting cushion into which she has settled so comfortably, these curves are gentle and softly coloured. In the fingers which hold up the book, the curves grow more supple; until, in the ribbons and bows and the ruff at the girl's neck, the curves run wild, twisting and doubling back on themselves, with the points of gleaming white where the sunlight is caught by a loop of satin. Fragonard must surely have enjoyed the dashing wrist-strokes with which these arcs of glistening paint were flicked on to the canvas.

Jean-Honoré Fragonard, *A Young Girl Reading*, c.1776.

A Roman at home

The small figure reading by a window is no ordinary boy: as the lettering on the wall makes clear, it is Cicero. Cicero is said to have studied hard as a child, before his writings and speeches made him one of the most famous figures in ancient Rome.

Frescoes

Unlike most of the pictures shown in this book, which were painted on to wood or canvas, this picture was originally painted directly on to a wall, the plaster of which was still wet. This method of painting, which is known as 'fresco' (meaning 'fresh'), was common in Italy in the fifteenth century, when Vincenzo Foppa carried out this work. The light, clear colours seen here are typical of fresco painting.

A casual leg

The Italians of Foppa's time were great admirers of the arts and sciences which had flourished in Rome many centuries earlier. They particularly respected the logical argument and balanced language of Cicero; and, suitably, Foppa has placed his figure of Cicero on a balcony which forms a framework of straight lines and carefully judged angles. In such a precise setting, this model character might seem a little too solemn and dull, if he did not have one leg swung casually up on the window-seat — suggesting that he is not merely a studious schoolboy, but is actually enjoying what he reads.

Vincenzo Foppa, *Young Cicero Reading*, c. 1460.

A cold shoulder

A long hop

After the cool, imaginary balcony of the last picture, Edward Hopper's harshly lit room in modern New York brings us sharply back to reality. In tone and atmosphere, one might say, Foppa and Hopper are entirely opposite. The young Cicero reads for pleasure, but the American seems to look at his newspaper only because he cannot think of anything better to do. He is home from work, but has nothing to say to his wife: she turns away, and idly plays a note or two on the piano.

Spy at the window

Hopper often walked along the streets of New York at night, and would catch sight of a room like this one, with people inside who did not know or care that they were being watched. By including the window as a major part of his painting, the artist seems to give us a similar glimpse of two ordinary people, who are caught off guard, in a typical moment of their separate and unexciting lives.

Many of Edward Hopper's pictures suggest loneliness: isolated buldings with no sign of life, or shabby rooms in hotels or cafés in which one or two people stare ahead of them. The couple in this picture are sitting only a few feet apart, but no longer enjoy each other's company. Each thinks his or her own thoughts, and waits for time to pass.

(Above) James Tissot, *A Passing Storm*, c. 1875.

(Left) Edward Hopper, *Room in New York*, 1932.

Storm in a tea-cup

The couple in the second picture have clearly had an argument; but we know from the title of the painting — *A Passing Storm* — that they will soon be on speaking terms again.

The artist, James Tissot, was a Frenchman who lived for many years in England, at a time when pictures which 'tell a story' were especially popular. This is just such a picture, in which the background explains what the figures have

done and are about to do. Tissot has painted a storm over the harbour outside in order to show indirectly that a stormy scene has taken place indoors also; and the patches of clearer sky are meant to tell us that the quarrel will shortly be over.

Nevertheless, it is not so much the double meaning which makes this painting attractive, as Tissot's sharp eye for details — the silver tea-service, the frilly dress, the iron railings of the balcony and the ships' rigging beyond.

Before and after

These two pictures show the same man, in the same room, but at different times. When the Scottish artist William Quiller Orchardson displayed the first, in which a man and a woman are sitting at dinner, it received such praise that Orchardson decided to paint another picture, showing what (as he imagined) had happened to the man and woman after a year or two had passed.

A world apart

The scene is a grand dining room. In the first picture, the husband sits at one end of the table, and his wife at the other, according to custom; but the artist has used the table rather as Tissot used his storm-clouds (page 23), to suggest that there is little affection between the two characters. Again we are given an important clue by the title, *Mariage de Convenance*: it has been a 'marriage of convenience', and not of love. The beautiful young woman has agreed to marry the elderly man only because he is rich and powerful. Now she regrets it. She has no appetite for the lavish food, and her wine glass is still full. She sits back, bored and sullen. Her husband, eyes downcast, is well aware of her mood; so is the butler, who looks anxiously at her as he refills his master's glass.

William Quiller Orchardson, *Mariage de Convenance*, 1884.

A sad old age

The second picture is called *Mariage de Convenance — After!*. The young wife has left, and her husband now dines at a table set for one. He spends his lonely evenings staring into the fire, brooding on his mistake, surrounded by the splendid furnishings which he no longer enjoys.

Many people admired these pictures for their story, or message, but others were more impressed by the way in which the artist had actually painted the picture. His favourite colours were brown and gold, laid thinly on the canvas, and with shades of these he created a beautifully mellow, slightly misty atmosphere, lit by the warm glow of gas-lamps or (as in the second picture) by the flickering firelight.

No tears for the artist

Orchardson portrayed the situation so simply, and yet so dramatically, that we might guess that something similar had happened to himself. In reality, however, he enjoyed a peaceful life at home with his family; and his daughters thought that, in these two pictures, he was trying to imagine a position which was the very opposite of his own. But in one respect Orchardson was like the husband in his pictures: he became an extremely rich man.

William Quiller Orchardson, *Mariage de Convenance — After!*, 1886.

25

Women in private

Georges Seurat, *Jeune Femme se Poudrant*, 1890.

Making up

A young woman, in satin corset and petticoat, pauses for a moment as she puts on her lipstick. Her name, according to the artist Edouard Manet, is Nana.

Fatal beauty

'Nana' meant a good deal to the French public, for it was the name of a leading character in two popular novels by Emile Zola, a friend of Manet's. In the first of these novels, which had just been published when Manet painted this picture, Nana grows up; in the second, which came out two years later, the beautiful Nana ruins the lives of several rich men who fall hopelessly in love with her.

A knowing look

We can only guess at whether Manet meant his Nana to be the same character as Zola's, or vice versa. But this painting certainly fits Zola's story of high life in Paris: the well-padded sofa, the fashionable Japanese screen, and the gentleman in evening dress, who has no doubt paid for these fine furnishings. While he gazes admiringly at Nana, she looks out at us, half amused and half sad, as if she feels that the events of her life are beyond her control. In Zola's book, Nana's adventures are brought to an end by smallpox. She dies in Paris, almost alone, in the Grand Hotel.

Woman of a thousand dots

The second woman at her mirror was painted by a younger French artist, Georges Seurat. Seurat took painting very seriously; he studied the science of colours, and developed his own method of building up a painting from hundreds of tiny spots of colour, each one carefully chosen to combine or contrast with the coloured spot next to it.

A puff of powder

Using this method, Seurat produced paintings which seem to shimmer, or (as this picture might suggest) look as if coloured powder has been sprinkled over the canvas. Yet Seurat's shapes have a solid, immovable air about them. Manet's Nana glances aside for a moment, but Seurat's large woman — whose unglamorous name, in reality, was Madeline Knobloch — seems as motionless as a statue.

Hiding the evidence

When he first painted this picture, Seurat included his own face (which he had never painted before) in the frame on the wall. A friend pointed out that this would indicate his love for Madeline — something which Seurat was keeping secret. So the artist was persuaded to remove his face from the frame, and to paint a pot of flowers in its place.

In the year after this picture was painted, Seurat and Madeline had a son; a year after that Seurat died, aged only thirty-one.

27

(Left) Edouard Manet, *Nana*, 1877.

Edgar Degas, *The Tub,* c. 1886.

An uncomfortable bend

Artists of almost every time and place have painted nude figures. Usually they have tried to make their nudes as attractive as possible; but this was not what the French artist Edgar Degas had in mind when he painted *The Tub*. Here a woman is shown standing in a broad, shallow tub, of a kind which many French homes used for bathing. Her position is not at all glamorous, for she has to crouch uncomfortably to keep her balance as she cleans the tub with her sponge.

Angles of vision

Degas produced several other pictures of women bathing or drying themselves, awkwardly posed with outstretched arms or legs. He also liked to draw horses as they twisted their necks and stretched their limbs before a race. In both women and horses, it was the angles, muscles and shadows of the body which Degas tried to catch. In *The Tub* the character or thoughts of the woman do not matter; we cannot even see her face.

Pastel colours

No artist has used pastel colours more skilfully than Degas. Sometimes (as in this picture) he drew on the colours with chalk-like sticks; in other pictures he added water or oil to make a paste, which he laid on with a brush. An unusual feature of this picture is that its brightest colours are those in the background. The metal tub in the foreground gleams more softly, reflecting the blue of the curtain, the pink of the woman's body and the orange of her hair.

An American in Paris

A close friend of Degas was the American artist Mary Cassatt, who worked for most of her life in France. Both of them admired Japanese prints, especially those by Utamaro (see page 16), and Degas encouraged Mary Cassatt to learn the method of colour printing herself. *Woman Bathing* is one of a series of ten prints in which she deliberately tried to follow the style of the great Japanese printmakers.

Japanese shapes

All ten of these show young women at home, doing everyday things such as brushing their hair, washing, or holding a child. In *Woman Bathing* the artist has not used shadows, or tried to make the woman and furniture look like solid objects standing on a carpet. The leaf-shapes hardly seem to be part of the carpet, but provide a decorative fringe as the cherry blossom did in Utamaro's picture. The gentle curves of the woman contrast with the sharp, straight edges of the washstand. Even her dark, pinned-up hair has a Japanese look.

Mary Cassatt, *Woman Bathing*, 1891.

Men of the world

Richard B. Martineau, *The Last Day in the Old Home*, 1862.

Drowning his sorrows

The Last Day in the Old Home is crammed with details from carpet to ceiling; they jostle one another all over the canvas.

The father of the family has been gambling and losing so heavily that he must now sell the country house which his ancestors have lived in for centuries. One ancestor looks down sadly from the portrait on the left. The portraits and the chairs have auction tickets stuck to them, for the auctioneers are already in the house, preparing for the sale and collecting the keys. The father is drinking a last bottle of wine, and has given a glassful to his son, although his wife protests that the boy is too young for it.

A full house

Nobody would claim that this is a beautiful painting. The many details give a fascinating idea of life in a wealthy Victorian household, but they produce a picture which is exhausting to look at. It would be a relief to find a corner that is not carved, patterned or furnished.

James Tissot, *Captain Frederick Burnaby*, 1870.

The hero at home

High polish

No other artist could match James Tissot (see also page 23) in painting the flashes and flounces of Victorian high society. Tissot's portrait of *Captain Frederick Burnaby* was painted only eight years later than *The Last Day in the Old Home*, but is a much finer picture. Its great feature is a seemingly endless leg — with a scarlet stripe, which almost links the officer's highly waxed shoes with his highly waxed moustache.

Man of action

One might guess from the comfortable sofa and the books that Captain Burnaby of the Royal Horse Guards was more at home in drawing-rooms than on battle-fields. But in fact Burnaby was famous for his daring exploits. Before he was twenty, he was considered the strongest man in the army; he was also six feet four inches tall (1.90 m), which may account for the length of the legs Tissot has given him. By the age of twenty-eight, when this portrait was painted, Burnaby had travelled widely, as a map on the wall and a rolled-up Arab gown remind us. Later he crossed the English Channel by balloon, rode in winter across central Asia, and was finally speared to death in the Sudan.

A matter of style

Tissot has surely painted Burnaby in the act of telling a story. We can almost hear the drawl of his voice as he describes some superhuman deed, which he has carried out as easily as he flicks the ash from his Turkish cigarette.

Hard times

Jan de Heem, *Interior of a Room with a Man at a Table*, 1628.

Scratching for a living

A scholar's life is less enjoyable than you might imagine — or so these pictures suggest. In each of them a young man sits with his books at a table, clearly unhappy with his situation.

The wrong choice

The first is a Dutch painting, as the black suit and white trimmings indicate. The artist, Jan de Heem, has given several clues which explain why the man in the picture looks so gloomy. The books and manuscripts on the table show that he has chosen a life of study; and

two swords, lying unused in their sheaths by the wall, suggest that he does not take part in the sort of activities in which a sword might be useful. Now, however, he has lost interest in his books. A portrait of a famous general on the wall reminds us again of the glorious military life which the young man is missing.

Panic in the attic

The Distressed Poet, as the second picture is called, shows a man who is not simply bored, but desperate. He is trying to earn a living as a poet; but his distracted expression is intended to tell us that poetry is not coming easily to him. He and his family are forced to live in an attic room – usually the smallest and coldest room in the house, and therefore the cheapest to rent.

No time for poetry

Nothing is going right for him. We can just read the title of the poem he is trying to write – 'Riches': a subject he knows little about. He is wearing a dressing-gown because his only suit needs mending. As his wife sews his trousers, a milkmaid bursts in and shows him the bill for the money he owes. His wig is slipping off; the baby is crying in the bed behind him; the cat has had kittens; a dog steals his last lamb chop from the chair right . . . No wonder he can't concentrate.

Actions not words

The artist, William Hogarth, was famous for his paintings and prints which picked out the less pleasant details of British life in the eighteenth century. Here his warning is similar to that of the Dutch artist, but is more sharply made: this 'poet' should go out to earn his living actively, instead of choosing a life which he is not fitted for, and which brings misery to his family as well as himself.

William Hogarth, *The Distressed Poet,* c. 1735.

A chilling dawn

Two more attic rooms, and still harder times for the figures who occupy them. The characters in these paintings, which are both set in Victorian England, are wretchedly poor; but they have found very different ways of coping with their situation.

In *The Sempstress* a young woman is sewing by gaslight. According to the clock, it is half-past two in the morning (or, since dawn can be seen through the window, is it ten past five?). She has been sewing for most of the night to earn a few pence. A magnifying-glass beside her shows that her work is already ruining her eyesight.

'The Song of the Shirt'

The artist, Richard Redgrave, painted several pictures exposing the difficulties faced by women who had to earn money. The wages paid for sewing at home were especially low (as indeed they are today). A popular poem by Thomas Hood, called 'The Song of the Shirt', drew attention to this miserable life: 'Work — work — work! Till the brain began to swim. . .' The girl in Redgrave's picture seems almost to have reached the point at which, in the words of the poem,

> . . .over the buttons I fall asleep
> And sew them on in a dream.

Richard Redgrave, *The Sempstress*, 1846.

Henry Wallis, *Death of Chatterton*, 1856.

The final flicker

For the young man on his bed, the days of poverty are over, for he has killed himself. He is the poet Thomas Chatterton, who has torn up all his poems and taken poison. As the sun rises over London, the candle blows out, and a wisp of smoke drifts upwards as if it were the poet's last breath.

Although this picture was painted in 1856, nearly a century after Chatterton's death, his tragic story was still well known. From a young age he had shown a genuine gift for writing poetry. He tried, unsuccessfully, to make his fortune by claiming that he had found some poems written in the Middle Ages — poems which in fact were composed by himself. Unable to earn a living by writing, and too proud to accept the food which his landlady offered to give him, he took poison. He was only seventeen when he died.

A deathly blue

When the artist Henry Wallis exhibited his picture, some people objected that Chatterton could never have afforded such gorgeous clothes as those in Wallis's painting. But it is the violent colours — the purple breeches, the vividly red hair, and the blue-white of the face — which give this scene its special flavour of agony and horror.

Musical fantasy

Below, a pleasantly festive scene in a Dutch dining-room; on the right, a picture from another age, made up of loud colours, swirling shapes and weird animals. At first glance the two pictures could hardly be more different — yet the subject of the second painting was borrowed directly from the first.

Hendrick Sorgh, *The Lute Player*, 1661.

A Dutchman's dinner

The Lute Player, by Hendrick Sorgh, is typical of many skilfully painted Dutch paintings of the seventeenth century. The man and woman have enjoyed their bread, wine and fruit (the peel can be seen on the table).

Most of the room is in the shade; but if we half-close our eyes, we can see that the painter has divided his picture with a line of light, leading from the sky outside down to the musician's ruff and sleeve, the music book, the tablecloth and the napkin (bottom right-hand corner).

The exploding man

When the Spanish artist Joan Miró visited Holland in 1928, he bought a postcard of *The Lute Player*, took it back to his studio, and painted the subject in his own way. Comparing *The Lute Player* with Miró's painting, which he called *Dutch Interior I*, we can see how he transformed the composition.

The lady vanishes

The broad diagonal of light is still there, but now it takes the shape of a huge white collar and a winding path of white linen. In the middle of the collar, like the stranded yolk of a fried egg, is the musician's face, fierce and red. Five wavy black lines represent his hair, and his moustache seems to have flown off his face, but his black beret is still perched above his head. The woman is reduced to a white bulge beneath the strings of the lute.

Carnival of the animals

The dog and the cat have kept their places, and have been joined by several new creatures (a bat, a frog, and a slug?) which hover about the picture. On the left we can recognize the river through the window, but now a fish and a goose are sitting on the water. The entire painting is witty, imaginative, and vivid — everything, that is, which the original *Lute Player* is not.

(*Right*) Joan Miró, *Dutch Interior 1*, 1928.

Returning home

Bernardino Pintoricchio, *Scene from the Odyssey,* c. 1509.

When a man comes home after many years' absence, his family may scarcely recognize him; and, as these two pictures illustrate, his return may not be entirely welcome.

The hero in disguise

In the first scene, from the ancient Greek poem *The Odyssey,* the hero Odysseus returns after twenty years of battles and adventures. His wife Penelope sits at her loom with a maid. Many princes, believing that Odysseus is dead, have asked to marry Penelope, and she has promised to give these suitors her answer once she has finished her weaving. But to avoid taking this decision, she unties every night all the threads which she has woven the day before.

The young man in the centre is the son of Odysseus and Penelope, who has been searching for his father. Nobody has noticed the bearded man at the back of the room: it is Odysseus himself, disguised as a beggar. He will kill the suitors, and finally reveal who he is.

The sorceress and the Sirens

Like *The Saltonstall Family* on page 19, this picture shows several events as if they were happening at the same time. Through the window we can see two of Odysseus's previous adventures. On the left he stands with the enchantress Circe, who has turned Odysseus's companions into black pigs. On the right Odysseus appears again, on his ship as it passes by the Sirens. Circe has told him that these creatures (who can be seen in the water) sing so sweetly that sailors who hear them remain for ever on the Sirens' shore; but Odysseus escapes them, by ordering his crew to tie him to the mast, and then blocking the oarsmen's ears with wax as they row past.

A Russian exile

The story of Odysseus is full of impossibly heroic deeds; but the picture above, by the Russian artist

Ilya Repin, *They had given up waiting for him*, 1884.

Ilya Repin, is all too real to many Russians. The man of the household has been sent away into exile, probably because of his opposition to the government of the time. His family have not been left penniless, as we can see from the wallpaper and the maid at the door. As the years of his exile have passed, they have grown used to living without him; indeed the title of this painting is *They had given up waiting for him*.

A shock for the family

The gestures of the figures are telling. The returning father hesitates as he enters; the maid

stands and stares. Only the boy on the right seems happy to see his father. The younger child's expression is suspicious – perhaps she does not recognize her father at all – and the two women in the room look more alarmed than delighted.

Couples

Pillars of society

If an artist is asked to paint a husband and wife together at home, how should he place his figures? Kings and queens in official portraits are often placed side by side, but less grand couples would require a more natural arrangement — one standing and one sitting, perhaps — as if they were spending a quiet Sunday afternoon in their garden or drawing-room.

Silent conversation

This kind of informal picture showing two or more people at home became popular in the eighteenth century, and was known as a 'conversation piece'. (The figures, however, were hardly ever shown actually talking to each other, because open mouths were considered undignified.) A typical example is *William and Lucy Atherton* by Arthur Devis. William Atherton had twice been Mayor of Preston, Devis's home town in north-west England; and in this picture the Athertons hold their heads up and their backs erect, as if proud of their country house and their position in society.

Personal property

In any conversation piece the surroundings play an important part, indicating the wealth and taste of the owners. The chairs, the clothes, the blue-and-white china on the cabinet, and the Italian landscape over the mantelpiece were all fashionable at the time. The dog, who looks eager for a walk, adds a homely and affectionate note.

David Hockney, *Mr and Mrs Clark and Percy*, 1970.

Designers at home

A casual toe

Mr and Mrs Clark and Percy, by the British artist David Hockney, is an obviously modern picture, with its smooth acrylic paint (a form of plastic) and its clear-cut contrasts. Ossie and Celia Clark, well-known designers and friends of the artist, are dressed elegantly but casually: if Arthur Devis came back to life, he would be horrified at the idea of painting the man of the house with a cigarette in his hand, a white cat on his lap, and his toes wriggling in the carpet.

Roles reversed

Devis would nevertheless recognize Hockney's painting as a conversation piece like his own. As before, husband and wife are placed on either side of a window — with the interesting difference that now it is the woman who stands and the man who sits. Again the objects in the room are used to indicate the taste and style of their owners (fashionable Londoners of 1970, in this case): the cream telephone on the floor, Ossie's flared velvet jeans, and the framed print on the wall, which is in fact by Hockney himself.

Even the airiness of the Clarks's room, with its plain surfaces and sparse furnishing, has something in common with the uncluttered interior painted by Devis. The Athertons and the Clarks would have felt equally out of place in the lavishly decorated Victorian drawing-room on page 30.

41

(Left) Arthur Devis, *William and Lucy Atherton*, c. 1743.

A fresh view

Conversation is another painting by Henri Matisse; here the outlines and colours are even less natural than in *The Painter's Family* on page 14. Nothing in the picture looks solid. The figures are like paper cut-outs, and the view through the window looks as flat as a poster on the wall. This wall is the same blue as both the chair and (strangest of all) the flower-beds outside.

Nobody special

In its composition, on the other hand, this picture follows a standard form: the form of the conversation piece described on page 40. The standing man, the window and the seated woman are positioned much as they were in *William and Lucy Atherton*. Now the point of a conversation piece was to record particular people in a particular place — but Matisse's

figures could be anybody; they have no expression; they are not characters, but patches of colour and patterns, like the balcony rails and the garden.

A break with the past

Why then did Matisse bother to use this traditional arrangement? Perhaps to make it all the more obvious that he was using shapes and colours in an unusual way. In

Henri Matisse, *Conversation*, 1909.

Conversation — which, unlike most conversation pieces, is a very large picture — Matisse demonstrated, as forcefully as possible, how an old tradition in art could be transformed by new ideas.

Rattle of bones

The Belgian artist Paul Delvaux has also used the basic structure of the conversation piece for an unusual purpose. *Squelettes en Conversation* ('Skeletons in Conversation') is one of several pictures of skeletons which Delvaux produced near the end of the Second World War, at a time when the thought of death was never far from the minds of Europeans. Yet this painting is not so much a grim warning as an artist's joke.

Not to be trusted

Once again the figures and window are in the positions that we have observed in the last three pictures. The arms of the seated figure are posed in very much the same way as those of Ossie Clark on page 41. The great difference, of course, is that Delvaux's figures are not a contented couple, but skeletons, who cannot have the slightest interest in each other. Even their apparently cheerful expressions mean nothing: it is simply the shape of their exposed teeth and jaws that gives an illusion of a broad smile.

Delvaux's painting reminds us that all conversation pieces are something of a sham. An artist can show two people near each other, smiling and seemingly close friends; but in reality these people may be no more able to communicate with each other than the two 'Skeletons in Conversation'.

Paul Delvaux, *Squelettes en Conversation*, 1944.

The artists in this book

Note: '*c.*', short for the Latin word *circa*, means 'about'; so '*c.*1440-*c.*1515' means that the artist was born in about 1440, and died in about 1515.

MARY CASSATT (1844-1926) left her native America to live in France. She successfully adopted not only French but also Japanese ideas in her art, as can be seen in *Woman Bathing* (page 29).

EDGAR DEGAS (1834-1917) was a French artist who excelled in drawing, painting and sculpture. *The Tub* (page 28) is one of his many nude studies.

PAUL DELVAUX (b. 1897) of Belgium has specialized in paintings of solemn female nudes or (as in *Squelettes en Conversation* on page 43) animated skeletons.

ARTHUR DEVIS (1711-1787) one of a family of English artists, painted individuals and groups at home: see *William and Lucy Atherton* on page 40.

MAURITS ESCHER (b. 1898), creator of *Hand with Reflecting Globe* (page 9), is a Dutch artist who has become famous for his geometrical patterns and effects which confuse or surprise the eye.

VINCENZO FOPPA (*c.*1440-*c.*1515) lived and worked in northern Italy; *The Boyhood of Cicero* (page 21) was painted in Milan.

JEAN-HONORÉ FRAGONARD (1732-1806) painted light-hearted scenes of gods, goddesses or French people amusing themselves, such as *A Young Girl Reading* on page 20.

DAVID DES GRANGES (*c.*1611-*c.*1675) worked in England chiefly as a painter of miniature portraits, but a few of his works, such as *The Saltonstall Family* (page 19 and jacket), have life-size figures.

JAN DE HEEM (1606-1684) was a Dutchman who painted fruit and flowers, and sometimes figures with books — as in *Interior of a Room with a Man at a Table* (page 32).

PIETER DE HOOCH (1629-1684), sometimes spelt de Hoogh, was a Dutch artist who is best known for his views of courtyards or spacious rooms, such as *Card Players* (page 13).

DAVID HOCKNEY (b. 1937) is an English artist whose great popularity is due not only to his paintings — such as *Mr and Mrs Clark and Percy* (page 41) — but to his witty and distinctive drawings and prints.

WILLIAM HOGARTH (1697-1764) painted what he called 'moral subjects' — scenes which pointed out the absurdities of English life. Most of these, including *The Distressed Poet* (page 33), were then published as engravings.

EDWARD HOPPER (1882-1967) of the United States first earned his living as a commercial artist. Many of his pictures show the bleak side of American life, as does *Room in New York* on page 22.

EDOUARD MANET (1832-1883) was the most brilliant French artist of his generation, although the critics of the time often disapproved of his paintings — such as *Nana* on page 26.

RICHARD MARTINEAU (1826-1869) painted episodes of life in Victorian England; his best known work is *The Last Day in the Old Home* (page 30).

THE MASTER OF THE LIFE OF THE VIRGIN was a fifteenth-century German artist whose name is not known. He painted *The Birth of the Virgin* (page 18) as one of eight panels of an 'altarpiece of the Virgin' for the Church of St Ursula in Cologne.

HENRI MATISSE (1869-1954) was the leading member of a group of French artists who were described in 1905 as 'Les Fauves' (the wild beasts) because of the violent colours they used. Both *Conversation* (page 42) and *The Painter's Family* (page 14) were bought by a Russian collector and have remained in Russia ever since.

JOAN MIRÓ (b. 1893), a Spanish-born artist, used his compositions of lively little shapes not only to create paintings (see *Dutch Interior I* on page 37) but also pottery and murals.

WILLIAM QUILLER ORCHARDSON (1832-1910) painted historical events and dramatic moments. He was born in Scotland but moved to London, where he painted *Mariage de Convenance* and *Mariage de Convenance — After!* (pages 24 and 25).

PABLO PICASSO (1881-1973) was born in Spain but lived most of his life in France. He did more than any other artist to introduce fresh ideas into twentieth-century art. He painted his version of *Las Meninas* (page 11) at the age of seventy-six.

BERNARDINO PINTORICCHIO (c.1454-1513) worked in Italy; *Scene from the Odyssey* (page 38) was originally painted on the wall of a palace in Siena.

HORACE PIPPIN (1888-1946) was one of the first black artists to be widely appreciated in North America. *The Domino Players* (page 15), painted near the end of his life, is one of his best known pictures.

RICHARD REDGRAVE (1804-1888) hoped that his paintings, like *The Sempstress* on page 34, would make English people more aware of the difficult problems faced by the poor. Later he became a teacher and writer.

ILYA REPIN (1884-1930) painted portraits and scenes of life in Russia, such as *They had given up waiting for him* (page 39). He was the best known Russian artist of the nineteenth century.

GEORGES SEURAT (1859-1891), the French artist of *Jeune Femme se Poudrant* (page 27), is famous for his majestic paintings created with small points of colour.

HENDRICK SORGH (c.1611-1670) painted scenes of everyday life in Holland, such as *The Lute Player* on page 36 and frontispiece.

JAMES TISSOT (1836-1902) was born in France but did much of his work in England, including *Captain Frederick Burnaby* (page 31) and *A Passing Storm* (page 23), which was set in Ramsgate on the east coast of England.

KITAGAWA UTAMARO (1753-1806) of Japan was well known in the West for his prints of graceful women. *Women playing the Shell Game* (pages 16-17) is a woodblock print from an album called *Gifts of the Ebb-tide*.

DIEGO VELASQUEZ (1599-1660) is often considered Spain's greatest artist. *Las Meninas* (page 10) is one of many works which he carried out in Madrid as Court Painter to King Philip IV.

VAN EYCK, JAN *(c. 1390-1441)* of the Netherlands was the outstanding artist of his time in northern Europe. *The Marriage of Giovanni Arnolfini and Giovanna Cenami* (page 8) has puzzled and fascinated scholars for many years.

VAN LEYDEN, LUCAS (c.1494-1533), who worked at Leyden in Holland, won a great reputation in his short life for such powerfully dramatic pictures as *The Card Players* on page 12.

HENRY WALLIS (1830-1916) was an English artist whose painting *The Death of Chatterton* (page 35) created a sensation. (Wallis's *The Stonebreaker*, an equally tragic scene, is included in another book in this series, *People at Work*.)

Finding out more

Books

Most public libraries and school libraries have a section of art books with good colour reproductions on particular artists, periods or styles. Take out those which include artists from this book or others whose work you admire. Apply a critical eye.

Art galleries

It is better, of course, to see the real thing. Go round an art gallery and study a *few* pictures — those which catch your attention or which have been painted by an artist you have read about. Art galleries and museums will give information about the pictures in their collection. Some have an Education Officer, and many arrange films and talks on art and artists.

Acknowledgements

The author and publishers gratefully acknowledge those who have lent pictures which appear on the following pages:

Courtesy of the Trustees, The National Gallery, London 8, 9, 18; collection Haags Gemeentemuseum, The Hague © Beeldrecht, Amsterdam and SPADEM, Paris 1981 9 *(top right)*; ©Museo del Prado, Madrid 10; Ampliaciones y Reproducciones Mas Barcelona 11© SPADEM, Paris 1981; courtesy of the Earl of Pembroke, Wilton House 12; reproduced by Gracious Permission of Her Majesty the Queen 13; The Hermitage Museum, Leningrad 14, 42 © SPADEM, Paris 1981; British Museum 16, 17; The Phillips Collection, Washington 15; Alte Pinakothek, Munich (Kunst-Dias Blauel) 18; The Tate Gallery, London 19 and *jacket*, 30, 35; © David Hockney 1970-71, The Tate Gallery London, courtesy Petersburg Press 41; National Gallery of Art, Washington, Andrew W. Mellon Collection 20; reproduced by permission of the Trustees of the Wallace Collection (John Freeman Group) 21; F.M. Hall Collection, Sheldon Memorial Art Gallery, University of Nebraska-Lincoln 22; Gift of Sir James Dunn Foundation, Beaverbrook Art Gallery, Fredericton, N.B., Canada, 23; Glasgow Art Gallery and Museum 24; Aberdeen Art Gallery and Museums 25; Hamburger Kunsthalle — photo Ralph Kleinhempel 26; Courtauld Institute Galleries, London 27; Hill-Stead Museum, Farmington, Connecticut, U.S.A. 28; Bibliothèque Nationale, Paris 29 ©ADAGP, Paris 1981; courtesy of the National Portrait Gallery, London 31; Ashmolean Museum, Oxford 32; courtesy of Birmingham Museums and Art Gallery 33; The FORBES Magazine Collection, New York — photo Otto. E. Nelson 34; Rijksmuseum, Amsterdam 36 *and frontispiece*; Museum of Modern Art, New York, Mrs Simon Guggenheim Fund 37 © ADAGP, Paris 1981; Tretyakov Gallery, Moscow (V/O Vneshtorgizdat) 39; The Walker Art Gallery, Liverpool 40; Galerie Isy Brachot, Brussels 43 ©SPADEM, Paris 1981.

Index